RHINOCEROS
SUCCESS

RHINOCEROS
SUCCESS

THE SECRET TO CHARGING FULL SPEED TOWARD EVERY OPPORTUNITY

SCOTT ALEXANDER

FOREWORD BY

DAVE RAMSEY

RAMSEY
PRESS

Dedicated to Mom and Dad,
who raised me as a rhino

FOREWORD

Ever since I was a little kid, I've been a fast-moving, hard-charging, go-getting kind of guy. I remember back when I was cutting yards at twelve years old, I didn't just settle for cutting one yard, getting paid, and then moving on to the next. I tried to line up clients next door to each other just so I could cut two or three at one time! I challenged myself to totally blow away the hourly income of my friends flipping burgers and tearing movie tickets for minimum wage. I've honestly never been into "minimum" anything!

So when I was handed this book at a success rally in my early twenties, I immediately said, "Yeah. This is me. I'm a Rhino." Rhinos are intense, passionate, and focused. Rhinos see where they want to go and start charging, knocking down anything that gets in their way. Rhinos get things done. I believe that you have to have a Rhino mentality to win in the marketplace. You have to be wired up and fired up to get something significant done in our culture today. How many times has one crazed, excited player in a football huddle turned the tide of a big game? How many times has a strong personality stepped up to a microphone and spoken life into a depressed and distressed nation? That's called leadership, and that's what Rhinos do.

But most people don't win, because they're mediocre. They make mediocre efforts and get mediocre results, and most of them are happy with that. This book calls them Cows. Cows are average, leading average lives, milling around in the field munching cud and keeping their heads down.

In the early days of my company, I decided that I wanted to surround myself with men and women who are just as focused and energetic as I am about the work we're doing. I wanted to run with Rhinos! We don't allow Cows to graze in our building, so I require every one of my team members to read this book in their first ninety days with the company. I want them to understand the culture they're charging into, and I want them to know what kind of people they're going to be running with.

Now, I'll be honest. This book is silly. It's even a little cheesy. The author, Scott Alexander, is a friend of mine and I promise, he knows it's silly. That's okay; this isn't an MBA textbook, it's a fun book aimed at lighting a fire under you! It's designed to give you a framework for understanding the Rhinos—and avoiding the Cows—all around you.

"Rhino" has become part of the vernacular of our company. We all know what it means because we're all charging together. I hope as you read *Rhinoceros Success* and maybe share it with your own team that you enjoy it as much as we have.

—Dave Ramsey

INTRODUCTION

 Somewhere, deep in the jungle where few dare venture, there lives a wild animal called success. It is rare and much sought after, but only a few ever risk tracking it down to capture it. The hunt is long, hard, and risky. There are many hardships along the way that tear at your heart and soul. The jungle brush throws up an almost impenetrable barrier. Bugs constantly bite and bore into your skin. Poisonous snakes, crocodiles, and other dangerous animals present very real dangers to your safety. The incessant, burning sun is your constant, relentless companion until nightfall. Then the temperature drops to near freezing and you long for the burning sun against your already reddened, blistered skin.

At times you feel weak and dizzy from exhaustion. Success seems at times an imaginary creature, impossible to capture. But you continue on, because you are too deep in the jungle now to head back without your prize.

Months go by, maybe years. Still, no sign of success. It is a clever animal, rarely exposing itself, always quick to flee should it sense danger of being caught. Success is so uncommon, so unique, and so challenging that you must have it! No other animal requires so much skill to hunt and capture.

As rare as the animal is, even more rare are the men and women who set up their own expeditions in its pursuit. You and I are part of that group who *must* have success. The rewards are great. We know that. We also know that the hunt is difficult, at best. We know the odds are against us. We know many have failed and few will even attempt the expedition. Knowing all this, we know that success is for us!

Success is not easy. It is a truly difficult animal to capture, requiring lots of work, quick thinking, desire, and persistence on the part of the hunter. This book is a survival guide for your expedition, a "rhinoceros manual" for your greatest hunt. Use it and you will not only achieve more success quicker, but you will also have the greatest time of your life charging through the jungle. Let's go! *Right now* is the season for success.

CHAPTER 1

THE ART OF CHARGING

 The secret of success is, naturally, becoming a rhinoceros. In fact, my wish for you is that you wake up tomorrow morning as a full-grown, six-thousand-pound rhinoceros! Imagine the look on your spouse's face in the morning, finding you in the bed. Oh, it is fun being a rhinoceros!

In fact, it is so much fun that you will be up very early every morning, including the weekends. No more sleeping in until the last possible minute. You are now a rhinoceros! The sooner you get that into your head, the sooner you will achieve more during your rhinoceros life. At six in the morning, when your "opportunity clock" rings, get out of bed like a rhinoceros—not a sloth! Take a quick shower, brush your horns, put on your rhino clothes, and get ready to . . . *charge*!

Take a quick shower, brush your horns, put on
your rhino clothes, and get ready to . . . CHARGE!

GET CHARGING MAD

The first order of your day as a rhino is to charge. Hopefully, you have something to charge at. You must have some goals that will add purpose to your life as a rhinoceros. If you have been getting up every morning to work all day just to buy yucca-yucca bushes for dinner and pay the rent, then it is time to get mad. It is time to get disgusted! It is time to say, "I have had *enough* of being a lazy cow grazing in the pasture day after day. I am fed up with doing nothing, seeing nothing, and accomplishing nothing. I woke up this morning as a rhinoceros. I am going to sacrifice the security and complacency of the pasture and live a rhinoceros life of excitement and adventure in the jungle. I am going to be a rich rhino!"

Get mad!

Who is going to argue with an irritable, disgusted, angry, three-ton rhinoceros? You will get what you want. Just *charge* after it! Vow never to go back to that pasture again. Forget your lazy cow buddies. Get out and meet new rhinoceros friends.

Charge!

ALWAYS CHARGE MASSIVELY

Charge massively and you will have massive success. How else does a rhinoceros charge, but massively? By being a rhinoceros, you are almost guaranteed success! When you take on a challenge, you don't approach it like a timid prairie dog, ready to leap back into its hole at the slightest sign of danger. You say, *"Damn the torpedoes!"* You give it all you've got, never allowing the possibility of failure to cross your mind.

You put everything you've got into everything you do. Shoot now and ask questions later. You are a rhinoceros! There is nothing you cannot tackle. Everything you do, you do it massively! From the minute you jump out of bed in the morning until you're back in bed for the night, you are charging massively. It is all or nothing with you. You are a charging rhinoceros with your throttle to the floor—full blast ahead!

TWO-INCH-THICK SKIN

Luckily for you, you've got that two-inch-thick rhinoceros skin, because with your "damn the torpedoes" charging, you occasionally catch a torpedo or two. Never mind. You are a rhinoceros! Your skin is so thick that you hardly feel them. They might knock your breath out once in a while, but you are right back on your feet, ready to charge again and madder than hell!

Yes, you are a rhinoceros and you can handle a lot of adversity. You almost enjoy taking the punches, because you know that it is toughening you up. The more successful a rhino you become, the bigger the torpedoes. That's okay. You are a thick-skinned, mad, charging rhinoceros, and the torpedoes will run out before you would ever go back to being a lazy old cow in the pasture.

Keep charging!

THE REAL SECRET OF SUCCESS

Before I discovered rhinoceros success, I was confused. I had, and still do have, a whole shelf of books promising the secrets of success. Some said the secret was to have written goals. Some said to dress for success. Others advised winning friends and influencing animals. Some preached ridding yourself of bad habits such as drinking liquor.

Well, I had and did all those things and I was still getting nowhere. Worse yet, I ended up working for a thirty-year-old millionaire who had absolutely no written goals and he dressed like a big, sloppy kid. He used the foulest language I have ever heard and he was no teetotaler. But do you know what he was? He was a full-time charging rhinoceros!

Since I first recognized that trait in him, I have unfailingly found it in every successful person I have encountered. Now I firmly believe that if you are a rhinoceros, you are almost guaranteed success.

Get charging!

CHARGE WITH SINGLENESS OF PURPOSE

A rhinoceros charges with singleness of purpose. All energy is directed toward the attainment of one burning desire. The reason you are so dangerous is that once you set yourself charging at something, nothing can distract you. And you never charge two things at once. You concentrate on getting your first target and *then* you fix your concentration on your next goal.

Never spread yourself thin.

A magnifying glass will not start a fire until it remains in one spot continuously for a certain length of time. If it is constantly moved from spot to spot, nothing will get warmed up, much less start a fire.

You understand this magnifying glass principle and apply it to your daily life. You keep charging despite the difficulties, because you can never tell when the flame will spark. It could be tomorrow or it could be next month, but you know that if you concentrate all your energy, you will eventually have a roaring blaze. Then you can go and start your next fire.

BE ALERT FOR OPPORTUNITIES

As a rhinoceros, you are always on the alert. You have to be alert in the jungle. Why do you think cows and sheep are not found in the jungle? They couldn't survive.

Your sharp eyes miss nothing and your ears scan the area

like radar to detect the slightest noise. You feel vibrations through your sensitive feet on the ground and your nose picks up any foreign scents. Your whole being is on the lookout for an opportunity to charge. You are like a cocked trigger waiting to be pulled.

CHARGE DOWN OPPORTUNITIES

Wait! What is that smell? Your great body grows tense, ready to spring into action. You slowly turn your massive head toward the direction of the scent. Your eyes watch for any sign of a real opportunity. Your ears pick up a rustling in the bushes. An unfamiliar scent drifts by your nostrils. You are ready to explode! Is it an opportunity or a torpedo? Your eyes stare unblinking, straight ahead. Your head spins with excitement and your leg muscles twitch with energy.

Suddenly, you see it! An opportunity! It sees you and like a shot, you are both off through the jungle. You charge full speed at the opportunity—three tons of snorting rhinoceros mowing down all obstacles in the way. Trees and vegetation poke at your skin, but you don't feel it. Your opportunity is in sight and you are gaining on it. It is a good opportunity, though the chase is long and hard.

You start to tire. Is it getting away from you? "Darn it!" you scream. "I am a rhinoceros!"

Your second wind comes and your rhinoceros eyes turn fiery red as the breath from your nostrils turns to steam against the cool morning, jungle air. Through jungle, river, and mountain you charge on, never letting up for a second.

Then all of a sudden, you've got it! Your opportunity tired and you have run it down. You make the kill and then rest a moment—your great lungs heaving, your legs ready to collapse, your skin torn, bruised, and bloodied—and you bask in the thrill of your victory.

RHINOCEROS FUEL

What is it, exactly, that turns a lazy, contented, do-nothing cow into an energetic, powerful, charging rhinoceros? There must be something responsible for the transformation—something that perhaps we can isolate, analyze, and use to our advantage. What would cause a rhinoceros to charge, sometimes against seemingly insurmountable difficulties? And what keeps that rhino charging? Why doesn't he quit raising a ruckus in the jungle and relax in the quiet pasture as a cow? What is it that drives him? There is no such thing as perpetual energy. Something is supplying the power that makes him continue to charge day after day. It seems to be self-generating. It never runs down. What causes such great motivation?

Well, you are a rhinoceros. You figure it out! Being a rhinoceros, you are after something, right? What are the cows after? Apparently, not much. But why aren't the cows after all you are after? They have brains. They have legs to move around on. They have ears and eyes and horns the same as you do. Can't they see all the possibilities of life? Can't they sense all there is waiting for them? Can't they see all there is to do, all there is to experience, and all the places there are to visit? What is it you have that they don't?

You are three tons of snorting rhinoceros
charging full speed at opportunity,
mowing down all obstacles in your way.

YOU BELIEVE IN SUCCESS!

That's right! *Belief!* Cows just don't believe they can achieve and, consequently, they don't try. They don't give it even one good charge! They see all the opportunities floating by them, but believe success is for a few handpicked rhinos.

They say, "We are cows. We cannot charge. There is no use even trying."

Cows will tell you that they are being realistic. But we know the truth. Either they are just plain ignorant and lazy, or they are trying to rationalize their failure.

SUCCESS IS YOURS

Success is there for anyone who will get off their butt and charge it down! You know that. That's why you are a rhinoceros. You truly believe that whatever you want, you can try to get it and your chances are excellent that you will succeed. You imagine it as being yours. You can taste the victory of achieving it. It is your belief that runs your motor. It is your belief that fills you with an enthusiasm to charge, despite the torpedoes.

Your enthusiasm electrifies your cells and makes them come alive. Enthusiasm is what prompts you to jump out of bed early every morning. You are a charging rhinoceros because of your overflowing enthusiasm generated by your belief—your belief that you can do it all and see it all.

Enthusiasm makes being a rhinoceros so enjoyable and it's why rhinos are fun to be around.

RHINOS ARE NATURALLY HIGH

Rhinoceroses have a natural zeal for living. They are so high on life that rhinos rarely have a drug or drinking problem. Rhinos don't need an artificial stimulant because they produce it themselves, naturally.

Research supports this. Biochemists have discovered the existence of endorphins, a morphine-like substance secreted by the brain. Anthropologist Lionel Tiger tells us that these natural opiates depress pain and seem to expand our awareness of pleasure. Scientists have found that jogging seems to bring on the secretion of endorphins, which explains why charging rhinoceroses feel so good about life. Their brains are literally flooded with antidepressants.

So keep believing. Keep charging. Imagine yourself reaching your goals. You *know* you can do it because you are a rhinoceros! Your enthusiasm will keep you charging.

Charge! Charge! Charge!

If your enthusiasm seems to wear down, you will know what happened. Your belief has waned. Keep believing in yourself. You have to. No one else can do it for you. It has to come from inside you. Believe and succeed!

CHAPTER 2

RHINOCEROS TRAINING

 This chapter covers the exercises and habits I have found are important to maintain a healthy rhinoceros spirit. Let's face it. If you were not born a rhinoceros, it is sometimes difficult to continue as a rhino in a cow and sheep world. You don't want to be "Rhinoceros for a Day." You want to be born again—only this time as a rhino!

IT'S ALL IN YOUR MIND

Your attitude is the most important ingredient in being an effective rhinoceros. If you don't really want to be a rhinoceros, you won't charge like one. You have to want to be a rhinoceros so badly you can almost feel your skin growing thicker. You can almost swear you've gained a couple of thousand pounds and your breath has taken on a strong, hot odor. You suddenly develop a taste for vegetarian cooking and, best of all, you have an insatiable urge to charge.

You are a bundle of energy. Every muscle in your body is twitching with excitement. You are after something. You feel that unless you get out and start charging it down, you might explode from all the excess power coursing through your veins.

You are a Niagara Falls of energy. With the power in your body, you could easily light up the city of Los Angeles. You are an atom bomb waiting to be dropped. All you have to decide is what to drop it on. Don't waste your energy on trifling matters. Don't let anybody or anything drain your juice. Make sure you are going after something worth your time. Think big! Rhinos do not charge at jackrabbits, atom bombs are not used for the Fourth of July, and the energy of Niagara Falls is not used for taking a shower.

Go after a rhinoceros-size goal, one equal to your potential. Don't underestimate yourself. Remember what Dr. Robert Schuller said: "It is better to attempt something great and fail, than to attempt nothing and succeed." You are a powerful rhinoceros. Run after the greatest goal!

DECLARE YOURSELF A RHINO

Before you do anything else, put this book down and go get two 3″ × 5″ index cards and a pen. Don't cheat! A true rhinoceros would charge right over to the drawer and get them. If you don't have cards available, get a sheet of paper. Now write the following on your first card.

I am a rhinoceros! I have a damn-the-torpedoes spirit! I am full of energy and I can't wait to get up in the morning to start charging!

On the second card, write a sentence announcing the fact that you have reached the goal you are after and the date you want it to become a reality. For instance, if you have always wanted to start a tap dancing school for rhinoceroses, you would write:

I am the successful owner of the tap dancing school for rhinos, which opens for business in July 2015!

It is important to state it as though you already have it.

Next, put these two cards near the head of your bed. Before you go to sleep at night, read them out loud. Do it again in the morning when you first wake up. Try to read them with feeling and belief. Put some emotion behind your words. At first you might have to pretend that you can't wait to get up in the morning. The important thing is to make reading your cards a habit. You can't skip a week and then read them seven times in a row. Read them one time, every morning and every evening. If you keep at it faithfully, by the end of twenty-one days you will actually be a rhinoceros!

TAKE ACTION

These affirmations will do you absolutely no good unless you combine them with action. Say you are a rhinoceros and *act* like one! Reading affirmations without acting on them is kidding yourself. Get in the habit of moving. Get in the habit of taking action toward your goals. Tell yourself that you can't wait to get up in the morning to start charging and then when the morning comes, *leap* out of bed and start *charging*!

RHINO PORTRAITS

Another good idea is to find pictures of rhinoceroses and hang them in your home as constant reminders of your proud heritage. The bathroom is a great place. It will give you something to think about while you spend time in there.

Make a new family album. Find a picture of a rhino family and claim it as your family. If you can find a poster of a charging rhinoceros, that is excellent! Frame it and hang it in your living room. Also, look for rhinoceroses carved out of wood at your local zoo. The idea is to constantly remind yourself that you are a powerful, charging rhinoceros. Look out, world!

Reread this book often. I hate to brag, but I believe I have the best book out on how to be a rhinoceros.

MAINTAINING YOUR RHINO SPIRIT

You just charged out of bed. You showered and dressed, and you are enjoying a hot cup of muddy water. You pick up the *Animal Daily* and scan the front page:

DOLLAR DROPS TO NEW LOW . . . WATER SHORTAGE PREDICTED THIS SUMMER . . . FORTY RHINOS KILLED IN BUS TRAGEDY

Don't turn on the television. They will have a film report on the bus tragedy.

How do you think this affects your ability to charge throughout the day? It tends to dampen your enthusiasm, doesn't it? Why subject yourself to this kind of negative stimulation? You have thick skin, but there is no sense in pointing a torpedo at yourself, is there?

Rhinoceroses do not make a habit of watching television. Neither do they spend their entire mornings reading about crimes across the country. Let the cows out in the pasture fill their knotty minds with the negative aspects of life. Do not ignore the negative, but don't saturate yourself with it either. Just as weeds grow in the most beautiful gardens, life will always have negatives to contend with. Watch that your garden is not overrun with weeds.

Instead, read books and magazines stressing the positive aspects of life or something educational. We become the product of three things: the people we associate with, the books we read, and the media we listen to.

Charge with rhinoceroses, fly with eagles,
run with cheetahs, and eat with lions.

AS YOU ASSOCIATE, SO YOU BECOME

Charge with rhinoceroses, fly with eagles, run with cheetahs, and eat with lions. Don't hang around with cows or sheep. They will pull you down. You are a rhinoceros! Associate with doers, achievers, livewires, and animals with positive attitudes and you will stay a fully charged rhinoceros. Associate with sleeping cows, sloths, or jackasses and you will become complacent and unsuccessful.

READ GOOD BOOKS

You also tend to become what you feed your mind. If you eat dirt and garbage three times a day, your body soon shows it. It is the same way with feeding your mind: garbage in and garbage out. Be particular about what you read. Ask yourself, *Will the information in this book help me reach my goals?*

If it won't, why waste your time? Read positive, stimulating, rhinoceros books. Did you know that there are books written by the wealthiest rhinos in the world telling how they got rich? The lazy cows don't read them—and they can read!

Learn to use OAE (Other Animals' Experiences). Today success is easier for those who go after it, because there is so much help available. Start building your own success library. You will gather profitable ideas from reading, and they will keep you in a charging mood.

It doesn't matter if you don't have the time or inclination to take classes. There are CDs and Internet sites dealing with every subject conceivable. You can literally go to college through the computer, but take the advice of Jim Rohn, who says, "Don't let your learning lead to knowledge. Let your learning lead to action."

In other words, *charge*!

PLAN ON BEING A PROSPEROUS RHINOCEROS

How does a rhinoceros get virtually anything he wants? How do you achieve wealth others only dream about? How do you live the most exciting, most adventurous, and most satisfying life? *Plan on it!* You stand an excellent chance of getting whatever you plan. Plan for nothing and you will get a big fat zero—absolutely nothing!

Plan to be a rich rhino. Plan and then charge and, sure enough, you will be a rich rhino. Dreams don't always materialize, but plans acted on are sure to produce results. Plan your dreams and then work your plan. Then you have a chance of making your dreams come true.

It absolutely amazes me how some cows think wealth is a mystical state that is somehow haphazardly and mysteriously assigned to only the rich. Rich rhinos are rich because they planned on being rich. Plan on being wealthy and you will become wealthy if you follow your plan. A plan by itself will be of no use. That's why being a rhinoceros is handy. Rhinos don't just work their plans, they *charge* at them!

Charge on!

PLANS DO CHANGE

Your plans are never going to work out exactly as expected. At times they will have to be modified. Don't give up if your plan doesn't seem to be working. Remember your persistence and your two-inch-thick skin. Make new plans. *Keep charging!*

Don't plan too many things at one time. Remember the magnifying glass. Rhinoceroses charge with singleness of purpose. If you plan too many things to charge at, your rear end might not follow your front. That could slow you down. Plan your attack and then *attack* your plan!

WHAT ARE YOUR GOALS?

Setting goals is part of your planning. Your plans should always lead to the attainment of your goals. This is the stuff success is made of. Rhinoceroses thrive on goals. They charge them down with an intensity no other animal can equal.

Design the life you want to live.

- Plan your *long-range goals*. What do you want to be and what do you want to do with your life?

- Plan your *intermediate goals*. What are you going to be doing in five to ten years?
- Finally, plan your *short-term goals*. What are you going to accomplish this week or this month?

An expedition of a thousand miles begins with one step. Get stepping!

YOU HAVE TO GIVE TO GET

The name of the game we are all playing is free enterprise. According to Mark Victor Hansen, this means that the more enterprising you are, the freer you are. It is the best game around, perfect for rhinoceroses. The only rule is that you have to give to get. What you sow, you reap. Simple rules, right? Right! The game is easy to win and anybody and everybody can be a winner.

Then why isn't everybody a winner? Why are there so many losers?

I guess they have never looked up the rules. That is all they would have to do. Too many cows are trying to go through life with a catcher's mitt on both hands. Write the rule down now, so that you will never forget it.

I HAVE TO GIVE TO GET!

The more energy you put into something, the more you are going to get out of it. This applies to every facet of your life—from making friends to making money, from running a business to running a family. Stop giving and you will stop getting. Your life is like a river. Keep the water flowing and you will be refreshing, life giving, clear, and beautiful. Dam it up and you will stagnate.

Give, knowing that you will receive back ten times as much. That is the way it works! The farmer plants a cup of corn and reaps a bushel. That's a good idea, isn't it? Give, and you will get results. *Give!*

SELL YOURSELF

You are your own product. In the free enterprise system, you have to sell yourself. If you want to be friends with the lion next door, you are going to have to sell yourself to him. To win a mate for life, you are really going to have to do some selling! If you are seeking employment, you have to sell yourself to an employer. The better you are at selling yourself, the more options will open for you.

Do you know what makes super salesanimals? Everything that you, as a rhinoceros, already have! Rhinoceroses make exceptionally fantastic salesanimals. Isn't that convenient? Success is so easy when you're a rhino! It is almost unfair. You are always charging. You are audacious, aggressive, and enthusiastic. Best of all, you believe in yourself and what you are doing. That is the key to successful selling. If you are trying to sell something that you don't think is super great, get something that is. Only then will selling be as fun and easy as it is supposed to be.

TAKE CARE OF YOURSELF

Are you properly packaged to sell? Just because you are a rhinoceros doesn't mean you have to smell like one. Who wants an odor like that around? Make sure you take care of yourself. Your body is your business and you have an inventory of only one. That means you can afford to take the time to take care of yourself. In order to keep yourself charging efficiently, make sure you get the best of everything. Don't put cheap gas in your Rolls Royce; make sure you eat the most nutritious foods available. You can't afford to be running on only seven cylinders. Charge on all eight!

EAT RHINO FOOD

Eat live, green, fresh, raw foods. Rhinos do not live on tacos and cheesecake. Do not go charging after a bowl of Sugar Crunchies in the morning. Stay away from sugar, white flour, meat, and fried foods. These will take more energy away from you than they give.

Learn what is good for your body. Get in the habit of regular exercise. Be health conscious and you will charge faster, harder, and longer. *Charge!*

At least twice a year, take off for one week and go lie in a mud hole. Do nothing but relax.

TAKE A RHINO REST

Give yourself a rest every once in a while. At least twice a year, take off for one week and go lie in a mud hole. Do nothing but relax. It is difficult for rhinoceroses to relax, but try. Let your motor cool down as you contemplate your game plan for the next six months. Then when your week is up, explode out of that mud hole and *charge!*

DISCIPLINE YOURSELF

Discipline is having to do something you don't want to do. As young animals, we all had discipline. That's why we are as good as we are now. Remember the kid who had no discipline? His parents gave him anything he wanted, they let him do anything he wanted, and he did anything he wanted. How did he turn out? He's a cow now, right? Discipline is good. Discipline makes rhinos.

But who is disciplining us now? No one! We can do anything we want, which for most animals is as little as possible. There is a scientific principle called *entropy* that says there is a tendency from the highly organized downward to the less organized. There is never an increase in order unless acted upon by an outside force. The principle of inertia also confirms this. *Inertia* is the tendency of all objects, including animals, to stay still unless acted upon by some outside force.

A ball will not pick itself up off the ground and throw

itself through the air. In the same manner, an animal will not get up out of bed and start charging unless acted upon by some outside force. That outside force is your desire, your motivation, your belief, and your discipline.

Rhinoceroses succeed because they are self-disciplined! It is easy to discipline others, but it is difficult to master self-discipline. Fat animals remain fat animals because they have no control over their eating habits. Cigarette smokers continue smoking because they have no control over their smoking habits. Cows remain cows because they have no control over all the bad habits that make them cows.

COWS SUCCUMB TO ENTROPY

Hey, don't feel bad if you are a cow. Decay and disintegration are natural! A cow is a perfect example of entropy—right along with eroding cliffs and corroding metals. Besides, discipline is difficult. Cow habits take years and years to develop. To try to change them now would be too much hassle. Continue to rot in your cow existence—devoid of motion, energy, and eventually life. Have a nice decay!

Rhinoceroses thrive on discipline, and it takes discipline to become a rhinoceros. New habits must be developed— like charging, audacity, and persistence. Old destructive habits must be abandoned—like procrastinating, complaining, and worrying. Rhinoceroses have self-discipline. You are the boss. You are driving yourself constantly. You are staying clear of this cow disease called entropy. Never let it get the upper hand. Always be aware of its persistence and do not let it get a foothold in your rhinoceros life.

YOU ARE IN CHARGE

Take control of yourself! You've only got one six-thousand-pound body to discipline. Take it and create the most efficient, most impressive rhinoceros the world has ever seen! You have twenty-four hours per day to devote to the task. Keep charts and graphs on your progress. Make it rough and demanding. *Charge on!*

Fine-tune yourself to a degree of excellence. You don't let your Rolls Royce get out of tune. You don't let its spark plugs get all gummed up or its air filter become clogged with filth. At least discipline yourself to keep up with your Rolls Royce. Don't let a car beat you!

Discipline yourself relentlessly. You are your own boss. Slap yourself into shape! If you are overcome by inertia or entropy, whose fault is it? Your own, of course! You are the president of You, Inc. Why don't you run your company more carefully? You are the leader of your own band. Why don't you get it together and accomplish something? You are the drill sergeant! Why don't you discipline your troops? *Rhinoceros!* . . . Left, right, left . . . left, right, left . . .

ELEPHANTS NEVER FORGET. DON'T YOU EITHER!

Now that you are a rhinoceros, never forget it. Be careful not to slip back into the pasture with the cud-chewing cows that quietly await their slaughter. When you find yourself in a situation that requires energy, action, and some risk, *think rhinoceros*! Wake up in the morning thinking rhinoceros. Associate with other rhinos. Always charge massively, don't let the torpedoes worry you, and live the good rhinoceros life!

CHAPTER 3

HOW TO BE THE WORLD'S HAPPIEST RHINOCEROS

 How do you like being a rhinoceros so far? Are you happy? I hope so. If you are not, I would recommend going back to the cow pasture. Better to be a happy cow than a sad rhino. Some animals are born cows. If you do not enjoy being a rhino, why be one? The idea is to be happy!

Rhinos are happy traveling to new jungles and meeting other wild animals. Cows are happy watching television or surfing the Internet. Rhinos are happy when they are charging at their goals. Cows are happy to lie in the sun all day chewing their cud.

But don't feel bad about being a cow. Somebody has to take the job. We need the manure to fertilize the rhinos' gardens, and we need the milk so that we rhinos can enjoy chocolate milkshakes. Cows in the country provide a scenic view on our Sunday drives in the Rolls Royce. Cowhides make attractive wallets.

Be a happy cow. Be a happy rhino. It is your choice. Everyone has a choice, you know. But just because your parents might both have been cows doesn't mean you have to be one. Take a walk on the rhino side. Be really happy!

Cows in the country provide a scenic view
on our Sunday drives in the Rolls Royce.

CHOOSE TO BE HAPPY

Does being a rhinoceros guarantee happiness? Certainly not. Again, it is your choice. There are happy rhinos and miserable rhinos. There are happy cows and miserable cows. There are happy bears and sad bears; happy aardvarks and sad aardvarks; happy lions and sad lions. Everyone chooses their own state of mind. Choose to be happy and you will be happy.

Love life! Love all animals, even cows. Love the blue sky, the stars at night, and all beautiful things. Love yourself, love your Maker, and you will be very, very happy.

IT FEELS GOOD TO BE A RHINO

Happiness is feeling good about yourself. Treat yourself special. If your hair is dirty and you feel ratty, wash it. Wash it every morning so that you never feel ratty again. Go out and have your horns professionally manicured. Look good and you will feel good. Feel good and you will charge. Charge and you will succeed. Succeed and you will feel good. It is a self-generating cycle of energy!

If you need to lose a little weight to feel really good, lose the weight. If you would like to be the happiest rhinoceros in the world, that position is open! Decide to take it. Happiness is so simple, yet some try to complicate it right out of their lives. Decide right now to be a joyous, cheerful, exuberant, friendly, loving, smiling, charging rhinoceros. The minute you decide to be, you are! *Congratulations!*

EXPECT A COUPLE OF ROTTEN DAYS

There are going to be days, of course, when you just feel blah. You are not going to feel like getting out of bed, let alone charging. You will feel bored, discontent, and frustrated. There seems to be a small handful of days per year set aside for this. You never know when they are coming. You just wake up feeling plain lousy. Don't worry about it. Hopefully, it will be over in a day or two. Ride it out the best you can and soon you will be your old rhinoceros self again. Then, continue charging!

NEVER LOSE YOUR SENSE OF HUMOR

Learn to laugh at yourself. It is really easy. Have you ever seen a three-ton rhinoceros filling out an income tax form? Does that make you chuckle? Did I see a little smile there? Well, you can let out a really big guffaw, because you will be doing just that at the end of this year! I can see you now, you big rhinoceros you, sitting at the kitchen table with perspiration dripping off your horns and your hot, muggy breath curling the tax forms.

I can see you now, you big rhinoceros you,
sitting at the kitchen table with
perspiration dripping off your horns and your
hot, muggy breath curling the tax forms.

Rather than get all bent out of shape paying taxes, appreciate them. Be thankful for being able to pay the salaries of those who sit and watch radar screens to make sure we are safe from foreign rhinos, as we charge around making money and being happy. Don't waste too much energy trying to figure out ways to cheat the tax cows. It is fun to make money! Just go out and charge down some more. Delight in the fact that you pay more in taxes each year than the cows earn all year long!

HOORAY FOR INFLATION

Thank heaven for inflation! Do you know how easy it is going to be to make your first million dollars with inflation? While all the cows are complaining about how much everything costs, you are out raking in all the dough! Sure, you have to pay a little more for gas to put in your Rolls Royce, but driving it is much more enjoyable now. The price of gas is keeping all the cows off the road. There is less congestion and you can zip down to the bank in half the time it used to take you!

THINGS ALWAYS WORK OUT FOR THE BEST

In order to thrive with the least amount of frustration and disappointment, you have to be firmly convinced that everything always works out for the best. Say that right now: "Everything always works out for the best." Again, if you believe it will, it will every time.

Isn't it funny how everything always comes back to belief? You have to believe you are a rhinoceros, believe you can reach your goals, believe in yourself, and believe in your future. The greatest rhinoceros in the history of the world said it something like this: "If you can believe, all things are possible."

READ THE BIBLE

Did you know that the Bible is the original success manual? You don't need to read *Rhinoceros Success* or any other book to learn to live your life successfully. All you really need is a copy of the Bible. Every answer is in there. Every success book is based on the Bible, only worded differently.

Don't worry about being thought of as a religious rhino. The Bible says that Jesus came so that we may live life more abundantly, and that's what we all want. That's worth checking into, isn't it?

"For with God all things are possible." (Mark 10:27)

He sure sounds like a good guy to have on your side, doesn't he? Put the Bible on your "to read" list. If necessary, sneak a look when no one is around. A good place to start is the book of Matthew.

CHAPTER 4

BE AN AUDACIOUS RHINO

 You are audacious! Your audacity makes you the charging rhinoceros that you are. This is what separates you from the cows and sheep. You are daring! You are adventurous! You are recklessly bold! You are a charging, not-afraid-of-anything rhinoceros! You have guts! You have nerve! You have backbone!

Every day you wildly charge through the jungle having the time of your life. You don't ask for anyone's permission. You just plow through, knocking down anything that gets in your way. The jungle floor vibrates and the trees shake as you boldly charge through. The cows and sheep can hear you laughing as a torpedo suddenly knocks you down. Immediately, you jump to your feet and start charging again, making new trails through the thick brush of the jungle.

GO FOR IT!

"Go for it" is your motto. You shout it at the top of your rhino lungs every morning. You are not afraid of falling, because you know that nothing can hurt you with your two-inch-thick skin. The worst possible thing that can happen to you is that you will get killed, and death is a negligible incident in your life. Everyone dies, even cows and sheep. Why worry about that? Your future accomplishments are what excite you.

Not even rhinoceroses make it to the top of the hill without slipping a few times. Even if you tumble all the way back down to the bottom, the cows and sheep can see you smiling because you enjoy the excitement. Today you might be in the depths of depression, but tomorrow you could be at the heights of ecstasy. You love the adventure! Jack London's verse really captures your damn-the-torpedoes, rhinoceros spirit:

I would rather be ashes than dust. I would rather that my spark would burn out in a brilliant blaze than be stifled by dry-rot. I would rather be a superb meteor, every atom of me in magnificent glow, than a sleepy and permanent planet.

AUDACITY IS ESSENTIAL

Choose to be audacious. Have an audacity attack every day. Success is audacious. Be bold and go after it! Develop your audacity skills. Do things that take nerve. Don't be obnoxious or make a jackass out of yourself, but do every daring thing necessary to reach your goals.

Every goal, every dream, every great project requires some audacity. If success were easy, if it did not involve some risk or the danger of failing, there would be no unsuccessful cows, sheep, or sloths. Success takes nerve. Rhinoceroses have that nerve. You are daring enough to charge down your dreams. Be aggressive! Not in a violent manner, but be aggressive in your driving, forceful energy to get whatever you are after. Aggressive, audacious, charging rhinoceroses succeed. No one is going to argue with you!

Charge!

DON'T GIVE YOURSELF ANY MORE EXCUSES

Rhinoceroses have no excuses. There is no excuse for not wildly charging every day. There is no excuse for not being audacious or not being on the alert for opportunities. There is no excuse for complacency. There is no excuse for not being happy and friendly. There is no excuse for not living the good rhino life. Too young or too old is no excuse.

Not even rhinoceroses make it to the top of
the hill without slipping a few times.

Wrong color is no excuse. Bad breath is no excuse. Being in debt is no excuse. There is absolutely not one bona-fide, genuine excuse for not being super successful. Take control over your thoughts. You control what you are going to become. Don't think excuses. Think rhinoceros!

Repeat after me: "There is no reason why I cannot be and do anything I want to! Why the heck am I sitting here giving myself phony excuses? There is no excuse! I am the only thing holding me back and I refuse to do that anymore! I am now a rhinoceros! I can do anything!"

USE YOUR TIME WISELY

You have only twenty-four precious hours per day. Use them or lose them. Time cannot be saved. It is ticking away right now! As you shower in the morning, time is ticking away. As you brush your teeth and horns, time is ticking away. Time cannot be stopped. The race is on! You are being timed right now. Realize that before time stops ticking for you and no one knew that you were even in the race.

Minutes are precious. They are the building blocks of hours, which are the stuff days are made of. Days quickly turn into months. Months soon become years and years make a lifetime. But it all starts with minutes. Waste enough minutes and you could waste a lifetime.

Rhinoceroses do not fall into this trap. Rhinos appreciate their minutes. They do not waste them in idle activity. Live each minute as though you had to pay ten dollars for it. Make sure that you get your money's worth. You can get more money, but you can't get more time. Be a rhinoceros and charge every minute you can. You will pay for every minute you waste.

BE A KID AGAIN

How are you doing now? Is your blood getting thicker or are you a cow reading this in the security of your pasture? Do you feel there is the chance you could become a rhino or are you fighting me? Sometimes cattle habits are hard to break. Maybe you feel too set in your ways to make such a drastic change. Perhaps you feel too mature to start charging around the jungle attracting attention to yourself. Surely you are not so old or dull that you can't get excited anymore? Never get that old!

Never be overly mature. Be like a little kid. When we get too serious we lose the real joy of living. The world's problems do not rest on your shoulders. You are not responsible for them, or for seeing that they are made right. There will always be trouble in this world. The Bible guarantees it:

"Man is born unto trouble, as the sparks fly upward."

(Job 5:7)

"In the world ye shall have tribulation." (John 16:33)

You might be thinking that these are not very encouraging words from the Bible. They aren't, until you read on:

"Be of good cheer; I have overcome the world."
(John 16:33)

That is encouraging! So don't worry about the world's problems. Have a childlike faith and believe that they will be overcome. Isn't it fun being a kid again?

GET EXCITED!

Get enthused about the rest of your life! Become the rhinoceros that you are secretly aching to become. Burst right out of that cow costume and slip into a brand-new, thick rhinoceros skin. At first it will be a little heavier than you are used to. But you will grow into it. You will become stronger every day, and in no time you will be charging like the best of them! Get out in the jungle and let everyone know you are there and that you mean business!

Charge!

CHAPTER 5

DEVELOP RHINOCEROS PERSISTENCE

 You never give up! Tenacity is in every cell of your huge, charging body. You have the invaluable strength to keep at whatever you are doing, despite the circumstances. You are indomitable! Nothing can conquer your strong will to succeed. Torpedoes, hurricanes, earthquakes, taxes, lightning, rhino poachers, and landmines will not subdue you. You trample every nasty, irritating obstacle that tries to trip you up. Your persistence bowls over anything that is keeping you from succeeding!

A TALE OF PERSISTENCE

When I started high school, I decided that I wanted to work after school for a veterinarian. I applied for a job at the local animal hospital as an animal technician. A technician's main duty is to help the veterinarian control animals being treated and keep the doctor from being bitten.

The job was hard to get. I kept checking in for about six months until there was finally an opening. I got the job! Wow! Most of my friends were dishwashers or box boys or didn't even have a job and I was working as an animal technician. And I made $1.65 an hour—almost unbelievable!

I showed up for my first day bubbling with excitement. The first appointment for the day was a box full of newborn puppies brought in to have their tails docked. My job was to hold each puppy as the doctor tied a string tightly near the base of its tail and then snipped off the tail.

I took the first puppy out of the box. Holding his rear end toward the doctor, I tried to keep him from squirming as the doctor brought the scissors to his tail. Snip! The puppy shrieked and continued whining as his tail dropped to the table, followed by drops of blood coming out of the end of his tail like a leaky faucet.

Immediately I felt lightheaded, but tried not to show it. The doctor finished sewing up the tail and then asked for the next puppy. This one was worse! He squirmed more, screamed more, and bled more. Suddenly I knew I was going to throw up. I handed the puppy to its owner and quickly ran to the bathroom. My head was spinning. I felt sick to my stomach and had broken out into a cold sweat.

As I sat with my head between my knees, I thought,

Darn it. I finally get this job and now this happens. How am I going to explain this?

After about fifteen minutes, I went back to the doctor, still feeling a little woozy. "I'll be all right now," I told him.

But things did not get better. As a kid, I always fainted when I got an injection. It was just standard procedure for me. Now I discovered that seeing dogs and cats get injections had the same effect on me. I had to avoid looking at the needle as I held the animals, otherwise I would become lightheaded. Just looking at a needle could make me weak. Before my first day was over, I also discovered that I was afraid of and allergic to cats. My nose was running, I was sneezing, and my eyes itched and watered. What a wretched day!

Fortunately I made it through that day without actually fainting or throwing up, but I came very close to it a number of times. At the end of the day, I was discouraged. I really wanted that job, but I knew I couldn't keep it because of my weak stomach and allergies. Then, that night, I had a dream.

NEVER LET GO!

I dreamed that I was on a small boat all by myself out in the middle of the ocean. No land was in sight. Suddenly a bad storm broke out. The rain came driving down, and the strong wind felt as though it might pick me up and throw me out of the boat. I wrapped myself around the mast on the boat and held on with all my strength as the boat rocked furiously in the waves. The wind grew stronger and I found it harder and harder to hold on. It was as though the elements were all trying to break my hold on the mast. The pressure was intense, and I didn't think it would ever let up.

But I did hold on. And then, in my dream, I woke up on the deck of the ship and the storm was gone. The sky was blue and clear and the sea was perfectly calm. I had held on through the storm and survived!

When I woke up, I immediately recognized the dream as a sign to stay on at the animal hospital. I continued to work there, despite my allergies and weak stomach. At times it was as bad as my dream had been. Fortunately, I stuck it out and outlasted the real storm!

For the next two years—every day after school and through summer vacations—I worked at the animal hospital. My allergies disappeared. I handled some of the meanest cats alive and I even took blood samples and performed minor surgeries like pulling dogs' teeth and cleaning out and suturing up abscesses. I don't faint anymore when I go to the doctor's for a shot!

The point is to persist. When you are in a trying situation, hold on. *Never let go!* Imagine yourself on a ship with the storm trying to shake you off. Do not let go, unless the storm destroys the ship and it starts to sink. Then it is all right to loosen your grip to avoid being drowned as the ship sinks to the bottom. Otherwise, persist!

When you are in a trying situation, hold on.
Never let go!

HOW TO BE A RHINOCEROS IN ALL ASPECTS OF YOUR LIFE

 Do you know how to make a rhinoceros float? Root beer, one scoop of vanilla ice cream, and one scoop of rhinoceros!

Remember this extremely funny, side-splitting, hilarious joke, because it will remind you to put rhinoceros into everything you do. Rhinoceros success comes from being a rhinoceros *all* the time. You don't play rhinoceros while you are working on an important project and then go back to being a cow when the project is completed. This is a full-time position! You have to think rhinoceros every waking minute! This is why the rhino pictures are important. The minute you forget that you are a rhinoceros you lose all your valuable rhino virtues.

Opportunity can slip away from you in a matter of seconds. A torpedo can knock you flat before you even know what hit you. Think rhinoceros every minute of the day so this never happens to you. Keep a pebble in the bottom of your shoe to remind you, if that's what it takes to keep you *constantly* thinking rhinoceros!

If you go rhino, you will immensely benefit in six major areas of your life—financial, work, family, physical, social, and spiritual. Rhinoceros success can be had in each of these facets of your life if you become a full-time rhinoceros. Let's take a look. The first is financial.

CHAPTER 7

FINANCIAL

 How are you doing financially? Do you have enough money? Never let anyone tell you that money is "not all that important." Money is important! Money is essential! Without money, every other facet of your life is likely to suffer. You can starve to death if you don't have money.

Money has a bad reputation because most animals don't have enough. To justify their lack, you will hear them say, "Money is the root of all evil" or "Money can't buy happiness." Both of these ideas are completely wrong. They are used only for rationalizing the failure to have money.

Money is not the root of all evil—*love* of money is. You can like money a *lot*, but never let it become your god. Respect money for all the good it can do. Have excellent plans for your money. Enjoy money and have a desire for money, but never live your life for money. Money is a tool. Use it properly and you can build a happy, satisfying life. Use it improperly and your life will be miserable. Don't use it and you will lose it. The good rhino life will never even have a chance to get started.

MAKE HAPPY MONEY

Money *can* buy happiness! That's why money is so valuable. What else would you want to buy with it . . . unhappiness? No matter how much or how little money you have, it can always buy happiness—whether it is paying cash for your twelve-room beach house in Hawaii or paying last month's rent on your apartment to keep from being evicted. If money can't buy happiness, why is everyone trying to get it? Poverty cannot buy happiness. Stay away from that!

What about the animals with so much money they could never use it all, yet they are miserable? These are the animals who have made money their god. Money can buy happiness, but it makes a poor savior. Consider the billionaires who have ended their own lives. Be careful you do not get stuck on this route. The best way to make happy money is to make money your hobby and not your god.

MAKING MONEY AS A HOBBY

You now have a new hobby—making money. It is right up there as being one of the most profitable hobbies available. Rhinoceroses love to make money! They love the excitement, the challenge, and the rewards of building a fortune.

Making money beats collecting stamps or old bottles any day. Become good at this hobby and you are liable to become wealthy. But make it your hobby, not your work. Wouldn't you rather spend time with your hobby every day than go to work? Hobbies are fun, entertaining, and stimulating. This is a hobby that will get you up early in the morning. You might not even sleep well because you are so excited about getting up. Remember Christmas Eve when you were a kid? That is how excited about waking up in the morning you want to be every day!

Making money will beautifully complement any other hobbies you may have. If you enjoy making money and flying, there could be a turbo-charged Bonanza in your life; making money and collecting stamps, there could be an around-the-world cruise to the countries on the stamps you collect; making money and skiing, you could one day own your own ski resort. Can you think of any other hobby more exciting than making money? Start your collection today!

If you enjoy making money and skiing,
you could one day own your own ski resort.

TRY TITHING

Always remember, though, this is only a hobby. Don't let it become your master. Never be afraid of losing everything you have made. Do not fall in love with money to the point it becomes a burden. If you worry about losing it, worry about it being stolen, or worry about spending it, it has become a millstone around your neck. In that sense, money cannot buy happiness. At that point, money has become your god.

In order to avoid falling into this trap, I highly recommend tithing. Give 10 percent of all the money you make back to God. After all, if he is your partner, he deserves at least 10 percent of the take, doesn't he? If he isn't your partner, sign him on as soon as possible. Where else are you going to find help like that at such a price? God has never figured inflation into his salary. He has been at 10 percent for thousands of years. He has got to be the best bargain around today!

Give his 10 percent to the religious institution that inspires you. Tithing fits right in with our free enterprise system: you have to give to get.

"Give, and it shall be given unto you." (Luke 6:38)

Many of our modern millionaires—including the Heinz, Colgate, Kraft, and Rockefeller families—have pointed to tithing as the key that brought them fortunes. King Solomon, one of the richest men who ever lived, said, "Honor the LORD with thy substance, and with the firstfruits of all thine increase: So shall thy barns be filled with plenty, and thy presses shall burst out with new wine" (Proverbs 3:9–10).

IT IS YOUR CHOICE

I started tithing when I was twenty-one years old. I had just expanded my own business too quickly and spent too much money renting office space and hiring people. When I realized that my bills one month were two thousand dollars and I could only pay about half that much, I felt faint and had to lie down for a minute.

At that point I decided that I needed help. I jumped out of the driver's seat and handed the wheel over to God. I started to pay him 10 percent of all the money that came in. To pay my first 10 percent, I actually borrowed more money, which put me deeper in the hole.

My wine vats did not overflow with the finest wines, but I did manage to climb out of what seemed an impossibly deep hole to ever climb out of. I continue to tithe for three reasons:

- Tithing helps me keep a proper perspective on money. I never want to be a scrooge. Giving is the most fun part of having money.

- I believe to keep someone good working for you, you have to pay that person well. Remember, you have to give to get.
- I can't wait until my barns are filled with wheat and barley!

But it is up to you. There are many wealthy rhinos that do not tithe. It depends on what you want out of life and what you believe. I can only present the facts and my opinion. I highly recommend tithing to live a richer, fuller rhino life.

ALWAYS PAY YOURSELF FIRST

Regardless of whether you tithe or not, you have to save at least 10 percent of all you make. This is absolutely essential! You have no choice here. I cannot stress the importance of this too much. The excellent book *The Richest Man in Babylon* by George S. Clason is required reading for all rhinoceroses. Charge to your bookstore and get a copy.

Learn to pay yourself first. Before you deposit your money, write a check out to yourself for 10 percent of what you made and then put it in a savings account. This is your rhinoceros investment money.

Start saving for your next opportunity.

CHAPTER 8

WORK

 Closely related to your financial picture is your work environment. If you are struggling financially, you are probably suffering in your work. No one should be *working*. Work means drudgery and monotony. Work is dull, irksome, distasteful, and uninspiring. Who wants that? Certainly not you, a rhinoceros! That sounds like the perfect occupation for a cow, but not for you!

Find something that you can really get your horns into and enjoy. Enjoy what you do every day or it will be work, and you will never be fulfilled working at something you can't wait to leave. You are not going to charge out of bed in the morning if all you have to look forward to is work. *Yech!* To be truly successful and make money, you must do something you enjoy, something you are interested in, something that inspires you. Only you know what that is. When you find that and delve into it, money will come to you automatically.

PLAN YOUR ESCAPE

If you dread each day because of your work, *get out fast!* Plan your escape. Make plans to get into something you really want to do. Do not wait for permission. You will never get it. Don't ask other people what they think you should do. How would they know? People will not want you to get ahead of them. I'll tell you right now what they will say. It will be something along this line: "If you quit, you are stupid!"

When cows call you stupid or foolish and when sheep tell you that you are going to regret something, you know that you are on the right track. Keep charging! If a lion tells you that you are stupid, proceed cautiously. If a rhino tells you that you are stupid, you *are* stupid! A true rhino would never tell anyone that, though, so don't wait for permission. Be an audacious rhinoceros and give your two weeks' notice to the head of the cow pasture. Your rhino instincts beckon you to the jungle of adventure and achievement.

If you are working at a job that you are glad you have, then show it. You can still be an effective rhinoceros. Employers love to have charging rhinoceroses on the payroll. They are about the only ones worth paying. Therefore, they are the ones who quickly advance in the company and receive frequent raises and promotions.

Show your boss that you are a rhino. Let your work be your challenge. See how much more you can produce. See what ideas you can come up with to become more valuable to your company. You will have the free enterprise system working for you—giving and getting. Give more of yourself and you will get more back. You don't get heat from a fireplace until you put in the wood. Put in your wood! You will command and receive the highest wages and conditions because you give more. You charge while everyone else is crawling. You help, rather than hinder, and inspire others to put out more.

DON'T BE LIKE THE LIVING DEAD

Be happy at work. Have you ever gone into a civil service building and noticed the employees? They are the living dead! When I went downtown to file my business paperwork, I couldn't believe the cows at the windows. They all acted as though they had knives stuck in their backs. They spoke in a monotone and never showed any emotion. It was chilling. I thought I had entered the twilight zone!

Be a rhinoceros and show your personality. Smile and act *alive*! Put some spring in your step and some warmth in your handshake. Put some feeling behind your words and show an eagerness to help. You will not only like yourself better, but you will create a warmer, friendlier, more productive work environment and everyone will love you for that, especially the boss.

If you want more from your job, show up tomorrow as a full-time rhinoceros. Don't worry about the rumors that you have been drinking or that you fell out of bed on your head. Remember your two-inch-thick skin and your audacity.

Cows hate to work with rhinos because rhinos make them look bad. Cows are lazy and unproductive. They will try to pull you down to their level. Don't let them. There is a loose rhinoceros in the place now! Watch out! There's no telling what will happen. One rhinoceros can really wake a place up. Decide to be that rhino and watch good things start to happen to you.

RHINOS MAKE SUCCESSFUL SALESANIMALS

There are more rhinoceroses in the field of sales than anywhere else. The nature of selling requires rhinos. A cow trying to make money in sales could live a hell on earth, but a rhino in sales could mean millions of dollars. We have already talked about selling, but I would like to acknowledge the successful rhinos in the sales world. You are a rare breed of rhino. Your species is bigger, more aggressive, faster, more audacious, and you have skin about *six* inches thick. They don't shoot torpedoes at you; they send out armies! There is nothing that can subdue a charging salesrhino. You are a powerful animal. *Keep charging!*

CHAPTER 9

FAMILY

 Your family can either make you or break you. How you do in your family affects your financial status and work environment, and your financial status and work environment affect your family life. In fact, all six major areas of your life affect the others to some extent. For this reason, it is important to keep them in balance. You don't want to become so involved in your work that you forget you have a family. They are your responsibility too. Rhinoceroses excel in *all* areas of their lives. This helps lead to happiness and contentment. In the end, that's what we're all after, isn't it?

Have a happy family life. To do that, just be your rhinoceros self. Keeping a family together and happy takes a rhino at times. There will always be times when things don't work out. Don't abandon ship at the first sign of rough seas! That's what cows do. Weather it out. Nothing good comes easy.

Involve your family in your plans.

A marriage is like a beautiful garden. It needs to be constantly cared for, nurtured, and appreciated. Watch for weeds and don't let them take root. Keep bugs and gophers out. That is your duty to the garden. Neglect it for a week and it could cost you months in repair. A happy marriage requires time and effort. Don't waste your time looking for one that doesn't.

As for kids, I don't know what to say. Having no children yet, I can only offer this advice. You are a rhinoceros. You will figure it out!

WORK TOGETHER

Involve your family in your plans. Make a fortune together! Rhinos that play together, stay together. Start the kids off right so they don't turn into cows during high school. When you have the whole family behind you, you will charge harder and enjoy it more. Take the whole gang with you to the mud hole at least twice a year. Help the kids with the new rhino math—or at least try to. Buy your spouse a nice gift at least once a week. Say you charged it!

THE SINGLE RHINOCEROS

If you are an unattached, full-grown rhinoceros and want to stay that way, be alert. You are in demand. You are 14-karat gold walking the street. All the animals in the forest have their eyes on you. When someone finally nabs you, make sure it is another rhinoceros. Then you can both charge off together.

CHAPTER 10

PHYSICAL

 Don't be an out of shape rhinoceros. Make sure you are in the peak of condition. A healthy body is required for living a rhinoceros life. You don't want flab bouncing around under your arms as you are charging. Make sure that you're not a few thousand pounds overweight.

How do you feel you are doing physically? A true rhinoceros is a magnificent animal. Would you describe yourself as magnificent? Extra pounds do not qualify for this category. Your skin is supposed to be two inches thick, not your fat. If you have more than you need, charge it off. Being physically fit will make you feel like a six-million-dollar rhinoceros. You can do anything! You are able to leap over obstacles in a single bound and you are faster than a speeding torpedo. You can charge your way to success!

On the other hand, if you constantly feel ill, if you are fat and out of shape, you are not going to produce in a rhinoceros fashion. If you cannot walk up a flight of stairs without getting winded, you do not stand a chance charging around in the jungle, being chased by torpedoes. Your chances of success are considerably lessened.

Put yourself on a regular program of exercise and get in shape. Train like a rhinoceros! Go all out! Charge massively! Don't do one push-up and five minutes of jogging in place. Do five thousand push-ups and then go on a one-hundred-mile run. And as you run, think rhinoceros! As the blood pumps through your head, tell every cell that you are a rhinoceros and to pass the word.

By the time the blood gets back to your head, every cell in your body will know that it is a rhinoceros. Your cells will be screaming, *"Go for it!"* They will charge out of bed with you every morning and you will glow from the eagerness of all your rhino cells rarin' to go.

Charge!

Get yourself in shape. A healthy body
is required for living a rhinoceros life.

CHAPTER 11

SOCIAL

 Earlier in the book I mentioned the importance of associating with the right animals. Now I am going to hit you over the head with it to make sure it sinks in. Here are some quotes that say it better than I ever could:

"He that walketh with wise men shall be wise."
(Proverbs 13:20)

"If you always live with those who are lame you will yourself learn to limp." (Latin proverb)

"When a dove begins to associate with crows its feathers remain white but its heart grows black."
(German proverb)

"Tell me thy company and I will tell thee what thou art."
(Cervantes)

"Chance makes our parents, but
choice makes our friends." (Delille)

Make sure you choose the right friends. We tend to behave in the same manner as those we associate with, and you don't want to start picking up some cow's complaining, some sloth's laziness, or some sheep's worry. Know as many animals as you possibly can, but associate mostly with the ones who help build you up.

And remember that *you have to give to get.* You will never advance socially if you forget this rule. To make friends, be friendly. As a rhinoceros, you will have no trouble here. You are one of the friendliest animals in the jungle, as long as no one gets in your way when you are charging. You enjoy being with winners and sharing the good rhino life.

CHAPTER 12

SPIRITUAL

 Only you know how you are doing spiritually. Religion is a very personal subject with most animals. Just the mention of it will cause some animals' hair to bristle up along their backs. If you are this way, all I can say is to believe in whatever you think is right and good, but please *do* believe in something.

> "Finally, brethren, whatsoever things are true, whatsoever things are honest, whatsoever things are just, whatsoever things are pure, whatsoever things are lovely, whatsoever things are of good report; if there be any virtue, and if there be any praise, think on these things." (Philippians 4:8)

Put the Bible on your "to read" list.
If necessary, sneak a look at it
when no one is around.

Believe in this, if nothing else.

And as long as you are believing, why *not* believe in God? It's not as if believing means you are going to have another monthly payment. Believing is free! You don't have to start going to church every Sunday. There is no obligation. No salesman will call. You don't have to read the Bible or even own one. There are no prerequisites for believing. Nothing to buy. You don't have to sign any contracts. If you are not absolutely satisfied within ten days, just quit believing! No one will call to find out why you cancelled. You have nothing to lose by believing, but everything to gain!

"If ye have faith as a grain of mustard seed,
ye shall say unto this mountain, Remove hence
to yonder place; and it shall remove; nothing
shall be impossible." (Matthew 17:20)

Rhinoceroses do not let opportunities like this slip by. Unless you can get a better deal, have a rhinoceros faith in God. I have found that he is the best bet around!

CHAPTER 13

RHINO GAMES

 As you drive about in your automobile, take notice of the other motorists. How do they look? Are they smiling? Do they look excited? You will quickly discover that our roads and highways are being traveled by a nation of zombies. Most drivers maintain a fixed, glazed expression as they work their way through traffic. Eye contact is avoided at all costs. Smiles are nonexistent. The only indication of any life is that their cars are moving. Somebody has to be pushing on the gas pedal. It must be them!

At the next traffic light, pull up to the nearest zombie and start staring at him or her. Study the expressionless face. What is he thinking about? He looks as though he might be going to a funeral—his own! Continue your observation. It's funny, but no matter how deep in shock the driver might seem to be, once you begin staring, he will sense it and look over at you, wondering what you are looking at.

Your tendency will be to look away as soon as the other driver does. This time, don't. Instead, smile or wave. This will totally baffle him. See what he does next. Most drivers will flash back a quick, nervous smile and then stare straight ahead again, anxious for the light to turn green. Isn't this a fun game? If simply staring won't wake a zombie out of his coma, beep your horn. Then when he or she looks over, grin the biggest grin you can and wave as if encountering a good friend you haven't seen in years.

Scoring goes:
2 points for a return smile and a wave.
1 point for just a return smile.
0 points for merely breaking the coma.
Minus points for any accidents.
Have fun!

TIPPING FOR FUN

Another fun rhinoceros activity is tipping. Now, I know there is nothing special about tipping. Even cows and sheep give tips. But they always tip the same animals. Generally, valets, waiters and waitresses, porters, and hair stylists get tipped. Look for other animals to tip. If a salesanimal goes out of his way to serve you, give him a tip. Tip the friendly cashier.

It doesn't have to be a large amount. A dollar will make the day for someone who has never received a tip before. Tip the waiter a dollar, though, and you will get a dirty look.

It is fun to tip people who are not expecting it. Of course, don't tip someone who does not deserve it. Tip the box boy who puts your bread at the bottom of the bag and you will feel like a jackass, not a rhinoceros.

CARRY $100

Carry at least one $100 bill with you at all times. Do not display it or spend it. Just carry it. Money is power, and having it on you will help remind you of your rhinoceros power. Don't worry about losing it or being mugged and having it stolen. If you do, you are a worrywart and you better have that wart taken off before it gets any bigger. You are an audacious rhinoceros!

HAVE A NEW EXPERIENCE

Every weekend the cows and sheep go out to dinner and see a movie. Be a rhinoceros and do something different. Experience something you have never done before. At least once a week, plan on doing something totally new to you, whether it be skydiving, roller-skating, going to an opera, attending a rock concert, disco dancing, or visiting an art museum. Taste a little bit of everything! Expand your horizons. Don't be an inert mass sitting on the sofa watching television like a cow. Remember, a rhinoceros life is an adventure!

FIND THE RHINO

Wherever you are, look for other rhinos. There are not a lot of them. About five out of every one hundred animals is a rhino. When you spot an animal you suspect might be a rhinoceros, go up to him or her and introduce yourself as a fellow rhino. Rhinos love to meet other rhinos. Do not be shy. Be bold! Hey, you are a rhinoceros! You have two-inch-thick skin. Explain that you are exercising your audacity, thank him for his time, and exchange rhino cards. Get to know as many rhinos as you can. Even rhinoceroses can use a little help every once in a while.

Experience something that
you have never done before.

CHAPTER 14

BE PREPARED FOR RHINOCEROS PROBLEMS

 Rhinoceroses are always prepared for problems. It doesn't matter how much money you have. You will still have problems. It doesn't matter if you are a rhinoceros, a monkey, an elephant, or even a cow. You will still have problems. It doesn't matter if you dropped out of high school or graduated from college with top honors. You will still have problems. Problems pledge allegiance to no one. They are for everyone. Regardless of sex, creed, breed, or color, you will still have problems. No one has ever been granted immunity from problems. They have always been around, they are around today, and they will be here tomorrow.

The rhinoceros difference is in the handling of your problems. A rhinoceros is not an easy match for problems. First of all, the majority of problems that would paralyze a sheep have no effect on a rhino. Little problems don't faze you. They are there, but you don't think about them. They are like gnats that buzz around your eyes. As long as you are charging, they are gone. But slow down to a stop and suddenly the gnats are buzzing around your eyes again. Keep charging and little problems are of no concern to you. They will always go away.

It is the big problems that you work with. These are problems that could stun an elephant. These are rhinoceros-size problems. You don't get sheep or cow worries. You get big, beefy, rhino problems. They come with the job. Fortunately, you know how to handle them. That also comes with the job.

PROBLEMS ARE A GOOD SIGN

First of all, you understand that most problems are a good sign. Problems indicate that progress is being made, wheels are turning, and you are moving toward your goals. Beware when you do not have problems. Then you've really got a problem! Not having problems means no action is being taken. No action means you are coasting, and coasting means you are going downhill! If you don't have any problems, double check where you are. You could be on the way to nowhere!

Rhinoceroses are constantly advancing. Problems are landmarks of progress. Pass enough problems and you will reach your destination. So expect problems and they won't surprise you when they pop up. Then go to work on them like a rhinoceros.

CHARGE AT YOUR PROBLEMS

The first step in annihilating a problem is to identify it. Do you know exactly what your problem is? Write it down. Put the problem in writing as if you were explaining it to a friend. This will help you sort out the real issue. When you know what the real heart of the problem is, ask yourself, *What needs to be done now to solve this problem?* Write down the answer or answers. There is a solution to every problem. Use your rhinoceros imagination!

When you know what needs to be done, get into high gear. Turn on your afterburner. If some charging needs to be done, charge like a rhinoceros! If it requires audacity, use your rhinoceros audacity! Whatever it takes to completely get rid of this problem, dedicate yourself to its extermination. This problem is your enemy. Let it hang around too long and it will cause you more trouble. Lower your head, point your horns at the problem, and charge full steam ahead! Tear it to pieces. Have no mercy. Take out all your aggressions on this problem that is keeping you from reaching your goal. Kill! Crush! Destroy! Problems stand no chance with a rhinoceros. Chalk up another one in your favor!

BE PREPARED FOR SORROW

Then there are the problems that you can't do anything about. These fall into the sorrow category. Deaths in the family and other tragedies are a part of life too. There is no way to avoid an occasional sorrowful event, other than spending your life in a closet.

Again, I have to stress the importance of having a rhinoceros faith in God. As great as we rhinos are, we did not create the world. We don't have all the answers. When times of deep distress overcome us, it is reassuring to know that we are not at the top of the line. Our Maker is up there waiting for us, and it promises to be a lot nicer than down here.

"Eye hath not seen, nor ear heard, neither have entered into the heart of man, the things which God hath prepared for them that love him." (1 Corinthians 2:9)

Unless you think you can hack it alone, unless you think we are the superior animals of the universe, unless you think death is the absolute end, believe in and love God.

CHAPTER 15

BECOME A RHINOCEROS TODAY

 This is the last chapter. If you have not decided to become a rhinoceros by now, this is my last chance to plead with you. Understand that it is not for my benefit that you become a rhino. You already bought the book. I have no medication or ointment to sell you after you become a rhinoceros—although that is a good idea and I might look into it in the future. But for right now, you are the only one to gain if you decide to go rhino.

All I ask is that if you decide to become a rhinoceros, commit yourself to it and go all out. There is nothing worse than a wishy-washy rhino. Don't make the rest of us rhinos look bad. Either you are or you aren't! Sorry I am being a little rough with you, but we do have an image to maintain. Well, what's it going to be?

LEAVE INDECISION BEHIND

Hopefully, you are not suffering from indecision: a disease commonly found in sheep. If you think you might be, but aren't sure, the best way to get rid of indecision is to become a rhinoceros. Rhinoceroses never suffer from indecision. Living in the jungle of adventure is a life full of decision, and rhinoceroses have no trouble making decisions and sticking with them, knowing that things always work out for the best. If you suffer from indecision, decide right now to become a rhino. Do not wait until tomorrow morning!

KICK THE WORRY HABIT

Maybe you are worried. Worry is a fatal disease found in all animals except, of course, the rhino. Worry is often painful and crippling right to the end. If you think you have come down with worry, *do not* put off becoming a rhinoceros any longer. Rhinos have nothing to worry about. We are bigger than anyone else—except the elephants that are good friends of ours anyway—and little things just don't bother us. Remember, we've got two-inch-thick skin. Become a rhinoceros and be free of worry. You will be so busy charging around you won't have time to worry!

Another illness related to worry is overcaution. With this sickness you will never have much. You will never achieve your true potential. Fight overcaution with your rhinoceros audacity.

Could it be that you do not believe? Could you be suffering from the agony of doubt? Maybe you doubt your own abilities and are terminally ill. Please, become a rhinoceros before it is too late!

Go thee forth, rhino, and
make your dreams come true.

DON'T BE COOL

Indifference. Maybe you don't even care! You could be suffering from indifference and not even know it. This disease runs rampant among cows. Symptoms include lack of ambition and "being cool." The worst possible condition to be in life is cool. Dead animals are cool! The good rhino life will pass you right by if you don't snap out of "cool." *Get hot!* Show some emotion! Let's see if you are really alive. This is a hard disease to kick unless you become a rhinoceros immediately.

Pessimism. Let's hope that you have not come down with pessimism. This ugly disease brings on complaining, always looking for the worst, and finally, getting the worst. If you have any brains at all, turn rhinoceros right now. You will be happier and so will everyone else around you. Optimism and rhino go together. The world loves an optimistic rhino!

You've decided then? You are going to become a rhinoceros? Congratulations! You may now proclaim yourself to be a full-grown rhinoceros, thus assuring yourself a long, successful, prosperous, happy, and meaningful rhino life.

Charge!

GO RHINO, GO!

You now know that the secret of success is being a rhinoceros. The secret of success is the overcoming of inertia. The secret of success is charging. The secret of success is to activate yourself. Get a burning going inside of you that makes you want to run. Nothing will happen until you do!

Think rhinoceros and *act* rhinoceros! There is no other way. Positive thinking will get you nothing, unless you combine it with charging. Writing out your goals is useless, unless you charge them down. Talking is only an oral exercise, unless you *act* on what you say. Dreams are only dreams, unless you become a rhinoceros and charge at them!

Go thee forth, rhino, and make your dreams come true!

Keep Charging!

ABOUT THE AUTHOR

SCOTT ALEXANDER is the author of three books—
Rhinoceros Success, Advanced Rhinocerology, and *Rhinocerotic
Relativity.* Written when Scott was twenty-three years old,
the rhino books have sold more than three million copies.

Scott speaks worldwide, presenting his unique and
humorous philosophy of success and motivation. During
the last twenty years he has been involved in such diverse
businesses as African art, fossils, and music. You can follow
Scott's continuing thoughts on the Rhino Revolution at
ScottRobertAlexander.com.

EVERYTHING YOU EVER WANTED TO KNOW

about building and growing a business,
but didn't know who to ask.